iMath
Readers

Ivy Sue Needs a House:
Building with Equivalent Fractions

by John Perritano

Content Consultant
David T. Hughes
Mathematics Curriculum Specialist

NORWOODHOUSE PRESS
Chicago, IL

Norwood House Press
PO Box 316598
Chicago, IL 60631

For information regarding Norwood House Press, please visit our website at
www.norwoodhousepress.com or call 866-565-2900.

Special thanks to: Heidi Doyle
Production Management: Six Red Marbles
Editors: Linda Bullock and Kendra Muntz
Printed in Heshan City, Guangdong, China. 208N—012013

Library of Congress Cataloging-in-Publication Data

Perritano, John.

   Ivy Sue Needs a house: building with equivalent fractions / by John
   Perritano; content consultant David Hughes, mathematics curriculum specialist.
   pages cm.—(iMath)

   Audience: 8–10
   Audience: K to grade 3
   Summary: "The mathematical concept of equal fractions is introduced as
   readers learn how to build a doghouse. Readers learn about numerators,
   denominators, and common factors. Includes a discover activity, history
   connection, and mathematical vocabulary introduction"—Provided by
   publisher.

Includes bibliographical references and index.

ISBN: 978-1-59953-559-3 (library edition: alk. paper)
ISBN: 978-1-60357-528-7 (ebook)

1. Fractions—Juvenile literature. I. Title.

QA117.P385 2013
513.2'6—dc23
2012023840

© 2013 by Norwood House Press. All Rights Reserved.

No part of this book may be reproduced without written permission from the publisher.

CONTENTS

Note to Caregivers:

Throughout this book, many questions are posed to the reader. Some are open-ended and ask what the reader thinks. Discuss these questions with your child and guide him or her in thinking through the possible answers and outcomes. There are also questions posed which have a specific answer. Encourage your child to read through the text to determine the correct answer. Most importantly, encourage answers grounded in reality while also allowing imaginations to soar. Information to help support you as you share the book with your child is provided in the back in the **Additional Notes** section.

Bold words are defined in the glossary in the back of the book.

Doggone It

Gather around, everybody. Ivy Sue is a Great Dane, and she needs our help.

Ivy Sue is coming to live with us for the summer. But doggone it, there is a problem. Cousin Clara is coming, too. Dogs make Cousin Clara sneeze. So, someone needs to sleep outside. I don't think Cousin Clara likes camping. So, we're going to build a doghouse for Ivy Sue.

Building a doghouse is not easy. Ivy Sue is one big Dane. Her house is going to be huge. She'll need to be able to turn around and lie down in it.

Everything I use has to be the correct size. If not, Ivy Sue's house will look like something out of a nursery rhyme. But I must finish before Cousin Clara arrives. Or *I'll* be in the doghouse.

Freaky Fractions

Before we start, I make a list of supplies. I need lumber, screws, nuts, bolts, and nails. All of these things come in different sizes. For example, sizes of screws and nails are written as **fractions**, or parts of a whole.

The top number of a fraction is called the **numerator**. It tells how many parts of the whole are being counted.

The bottom number of the fraction is called the **denominator**. It tells how many equal parts are in the whole.

Equivalent fractions are two or more fractions that look different but have the same value.

Let's say I have one nail and one screw. The nail is labeled $\frac{1}{4}$ inch. The screw is labeled $\frac{3}{12}$ inch. Are they equivalent in size? There are different ways to find out.

Idea 1: We can compare **fraction bars.**

One Whole											
$\frac{1}{2}$						$\frac{1}{2}$					
$\frac{1}{3}$				$\frac{1}{3}$				$\frac{1}{3}$			
$\frac{1}{4}$			$\frac{1}{4}$			$\frac{1}{4}$			$\frac{1}{4}$		
$\frac{1}{5}$		$\frac{1}{5}$		$\frac{1}{5}$		$\frac{1}{5}$			$\frac{1}{5}$		
$\frac{1}{6}$		$\frac{1}{6}$		$\frac{1}{6}$		$\frac{1}{6}$		$\frac{1}{6}$		$\frac{1}{6}$	
$\frac{1}{8}$		$\frac{1}{8}$	$\frac{1}{8}$		$\frac{1}{8}$	$\frac{1}{8}$		$\frac{1}{8}$	$\frac{1}{8}$		$\frac{1}{8}$
$\frac{1}{10}$	$\frac{1}{10}$	$\frac{1}{10}$	$\frac{1}{10}$	$\frac{1}{10}$	$\frac{1}{10}$	$\frac{1}{10}$	$\frac{1}{10}$	$\frac{1}{10}$	$\frac{1}{10}$		
$\frac{1}{12}$	$\frac{1}{12}$	$\frac{1}{12}$	$\frac{1}{12}$	$\frac{1}{12}$	$\frac{1}{12}$	$\frac{1}{12}$	$\frac{1}{12}$	$\frac{1}{12}$	$\frac{1}{12}$	$\frac{1}{12}$	$\frac{1}{12}$

$\frac{1}{4}$			$\frac{1}{4}$			$\frac{1}{4}$			$\frac{1}{4}$		
$\frac{1}{12}$	$\frac{1}{12}$	$\frac{1}{12}$	$\frac{1}{12}$	$\frac{1}{12}$	$\frac{1}{12}$	$\frac{1}{12}$	$\frac{1}{12}$	$\frac{1}{12}$	$\frac{1}{12}$	$\frac{1}{12}$	$\frac{1}{12}$

Yes, $\frac{1}{4}$ and $\frac{3}{12}$ are equivalent fractions.

Is using fraction bars a good way to find out whether fractions are equivalent? Why or why not?

Idea 2: We can compare **fraction lines**.

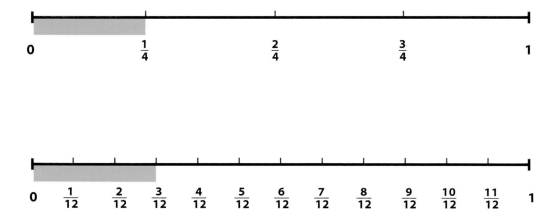

Yes, $\frac{1}{4}$ and $\frac{3}{12}$ are equivalent fractions.

Is using fraction lines a good way to find out whether fractions are equivalent? Why or why not?

Idea 3: Use **fraction circles** to model each fraction. Draw two circles.

Divide one circle into 4 equal parts.

Divide the second circle into 12 equal parts.

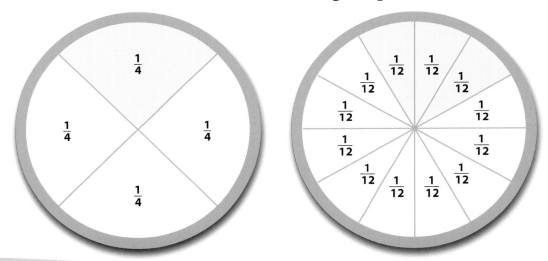

Compare the shaded areas. Yes, $\frac{1}{4}$ and $\frac{3}{12}$ are equivalent fractions.

Is using fraction circles a good way to find out whether fractions are equivalent? Why or why not?

DISCOVER ACTIVITY

Materials

- a collection of objects
- a ruler
- paper
- pencil

Equivalent Lengths

Look for at least five objects in your house. The objects should be easy to measure with a ruler.

Write the name of each object in a chart like the one below.

Measure the length of each object to the nearest $\frac{1}{4}$ inch. Write your measurements in your chart. Look at the example.

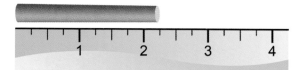

Object	Length
stick of purple chalk	$2\frac{1}{4}$ inches
_____	_____

How will you compare measurements? Will you:
- use fraction bars?
- use fraction lines?
- use fraction circles?

Rewrite your list in order, starting with the longest measurement and ending with the shortest.

Gentle Giants

Ivy Sue is the biggest dog I have ever seen. I think it would take two Labrador Retrievers to equal one Ivy Sue.

Ivy Sue is a Great Dane, but Great Danes don't come from Denmark. Denmark is the home of Danish people. Great Danes come from Germany. They're hunting dogs. Long ago, people used Great Danes to hunt wild boars. Boars are wild pigs.

Great Danes can also be great guard dogs. But only if they're not sleeping. Ivy Sue sleeps a lot. When she visits my house, she usually sleeps in my bed.

Great Danes enjoy a good rest.

A Great Dane's size and bark are enough to frighten burglars away. But barking is work, and Great Danes don't like to work. At least Ivy Sue doesn't.

Sophie, however, *is* a hard worker. Sophie is the cat who lives next door. She hunts, and she chases sticks and balls. Ivy Sue won't even chase the cat. Ivy Sue gets along with everyone.

Other than sleeping, Ivy Sue enjoys eating. She eats about 5 cups of food a day. I soak her food in water to get rid of gases from the food. Otherwise, gases collect in Ivy Sue's stomach. This can make Ivy Sue and all Great Danes very sick.

Before I go to a hardware store, I need a list. It must have every possible thing I might need. After all, once I start building, I don't want to stop.

I put lumber at the top of my list. I need boards that are $\frac{1}{2}$ inch wide, $\frac{1}{4}$ inch wide, $\frac{1}{3}$ inch wide, and $\frac{2}{3}$ inch wide.

Shopping for lumber will be easier if I order the boards from the least wide to the most wide. What order should I put the boards in? Use fraction bars to help you find the answer.

The Mighty Screw

A screw is a simple machine. We couldn't build a house—not even for Ivy Sue—without screws. We couldn't build a bridge. We couldn't build a car. We couldn't build a skyscraper.

What makes the simple screw so mighty? Screws have threads. Threads are the parts of a screw that wrap around the length of the screw. What happens when you drive a screw into a piece of wood? The threads grab onto the wood and won't let go.

Why? The width of the threads and the distance between them make a screw strong. The closer and wider the threads, the stronger the screw's grip will be.

The more threads a screw has, the harder it is to turn. To drive a screw into a piece of wood or metal, you have to turn its head with a screwdriver.

This **line plot** shows how many and what sizes of screws are in my toolbox. The fractions below the line show the different sizes of screws. The *x* above each size represents one screw.

How many $\frac{1}{4}$ inch screws do I have? What size screw do I have the least of? What size screw do I have the most of?

Screws in My Toolbox

The hardware store has many more screws than I have. They come in more sizes, too. There are $\frac{2}{3}$ inch screws in Box A. There are $\frac{6}{8}$ inch screws in Box B. And there are $\frac{4}{6}$ inch screws in Box C. Which two boxes hold screws of equivalent size? Use fraction lines to find the answer.

This is an example of an Archimedes Water Screw.

Connecting to History

Most people use screws to fasten pieces of wood or metal. But a long time ago, people used screws to water their gardens. Sailors used screws to pump water out of the bottom of their ships.

These gardeners and sailors used a water screw. A mathematician named Archimedes invented it about 2,700 years ago. The water screw was very simple. It was a hollow tree with a brass screw inside. The screw was attached to a hand crank. As workers turned the crank, they also turned the screw. The screw scooped up water and moved it up the hollow tree.

Sennacherib was a king of Assyria. He made one of the most famous water screws. His empire included much of what we call the Middle East and Turkey. The king built a great palace at a place called Nineveh. Nineveh was located on the Tigris River in what is today Iraq.

Sennacherib made Nineveh magnificent. Parks and fields of fruit trees were inside the palace's walls. The city had streets and town squares.

Today, parts of the city of Mosul cover Ninevah.

Because Nineveh was in the desert, there wasn't much water to **irrigate** the plants of the city's wonderful gardens. So, Sennacherib dug 18 canals to bring water from the hills six miles away. He used a water screw to pump water from the canals into the palace.

Imagine Sennacherib's palace was $\frac{4}{5}$ of a mile from a canal. Which two of the following fractions are equivalent to $\frac{4}{5}$? Use fraction circles to find the answer.

$$\frac{3}{6} \qquad \frac{5}{8} \qquad \frac{8}{10} \qquad \frac{12}{15}$$

Pressing Innovations

Before the mid-1400s, there was only one way to print a book. That was by hand. It wasn't the easiest way to make a book. A **scribe** would dip a quill into ink. He wrote only a few words before the quill ran dry. The scribe dipped again, and again, and again.

Then, in 1440, German inventor Johannes Gutenberg built the first printing press. Gutenberg used moveable metal blocks called type. Each block of type had a raised letter or number. Gutenberg arranged the blocks to form words and sentences.

He then put the blocks in the frame of the press. He rolled ink over the type. He put a piece of paper on top of the inked type. Then, he turned a huge screw. The screw pressed the block of wood against the paper, creating a printed page. Gutenberg could print as many pages as he wanted.

This drawing shows printers using a Gutenberg press in the 1800s.

The printing press provided a fast way to broadcast news. It also allowed everyone to read the ideas of other people. In many cases, those ideas started **revolutions**, or changes in government. As ideas spread, people sought change.

At first, most people didn't like printed books. They didn't understand the power of Gutenberg's press. But by the end of the 15th century, printers had printed between 8 and 10 million copies of more than 40,000 book titles.

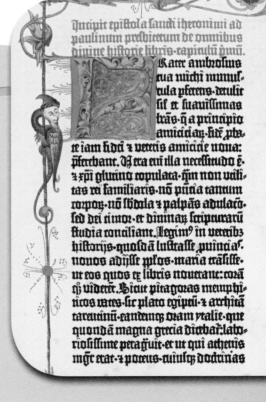

This page comes from a book printed on a Gutenberg press in 1455.

Imagine a library in 15th century Germany. Of all of the books in the library, $\frac{2}{4}$ were printed by hand. And $\frac{1}{2}$ were printed on a printing press. Are there more hand-printed or machine-printed books? How will you find the answer?

Nifty Nails

Nails are like screws. They're great for holding things together. Nails have a metal **shank**. At the top of the shank is a head, the place that receives a hammer's blow. The shank narrows to a point. This point is driven into wood.

Who invented these tiny fasteners? No one knows. People began using nails to build their homes long ago. The first nails were made from wood.

Today, blacksmiths continue to forge metals. This blacksmith is making a horseshoe. Blacksmiths who make shoes for horses are called farriers.

About 2,000 years ago, in ancient Rome, builders used nails to build forts. Roman blacksmiths heated and shaped iron to make individual nails. By the 1600s, people used machines to make nails. But they still made them one at a time. By the late 1700s or early 1800s, people were using machines that could make more nails at one time. The nails were called cut nails, and they came in a variety of sizes.

Today, nails are made of steel, brass, and other metals. Some nails are specially coated to keep them from rusting. The heads of the nails come in various shapes, depending on the nail's job. Carpenters use small-head finishing nails for delicate work. Roofers use large-head roofing nails to attach shingles to a house. Nearly 300 different kinds of nails are made in the United States. Carpenters use between 20,000 and 30,000 nails to build an average-sized wooden house.

What's the Word?

Nails come in penny sizes, with a number and the letter d. The letter is an abbreviation for pennyweight, a term created in England in the 1700s. Originally, a penny size described the cost of 100 nails. A short nail, like a 2d, cost less per 100 nails than a long nail, like a 12d.

I have one bag of screws and another bag of nails. Each bag holds the same amount. Until I drop them, that is.

$\frac{3}{4}$ of the screws fall out of their bag. $\frac{2}{8}$ of the nails fall out of their bag. Did more screws or nails fall out of their bag?

Hammer Time

Rap, rap, rap. That's all I've been doing. Drive a nail here. Drive a nail there. Sometimes I wish Ivy Sue were a Chihuahua. Chihuahuas don't live in big houses.

Thank goodness for my hammer. It lets me drive nails into wood easily. Hammers were one of the first tools humans created.

While I am hammering the roof to Ivy Sue's house, I run out of nails. I go into the garage to look for more. I want the widest nails possible. Should I use $\frac{5}{8}$ inch nails or $\frac{3}{4}$ inch nails? Here's a hint: Rewrite $\frac{3}{4}$ as an equivalent fraction with 8 in the denominator.

22

Lunch Time

Whew! Building a doghouse is a lot of work. I've been at it all day. Ivy Sue has not. She's been sleeping in the shade. She's a lucky girl.

Ivy Sue's house is almost finished. Now it's time for lunch. Lunch is my favorite time of the day. Pizza is my favorite food. And pepperoni pizza is my favorite pizza. Cousin Clara doesn't like pepperoni.
So, I order a mushroom pizza for her.

This pizza is cut into 6 equal parts.

Both pizzas are exactly the same size. I cut mine into 6 equal slices. She cuts hers into 12 equal pieces.

I eat $\frac{3}{6}$ of my pizza. She eats $\frac{6}{12}$ of hers.
Who has eaten more pizza?

Brownie Round Up

That pizza was sure tasty. Now it's time for dessert.

Cousin Clara made brownies before she came. She brought them with her. Lucky me!

Cousin Clara has cut 16 brownies of equal size. I eat $\frac{2}{16}$ of the brownies. She eats $\frac{1}{8}$. Who has eaten more brownies?

I can't think of a better way to celebrate our work than with brownies. I think Ivy Sue deserves a treat, too. But it won't be brownies. I have something else in mind for her.

Math at Work

Plumbers are very good at using fractions. They have to be. For one thing, plumbers have to know what size pipe to use. The size of a pipe is determined by its **diameter**. The diameter is the length from one side of the pipe to the other, through the center of the pipe. If two pipes don't fit, it could result in a gushing disaster!

Plumbers fix leaky faucets. They fix showers and toilets, bathtubs, and garden hoses. They use math to keep the water running.

There it is. It's finished. Ivy Sue has a great new doghouse. And Sophie, our neighbor's cat, seems to like it, too. I did a good job. Cousin Clara helped.

"Why don't we paint it?" Cousin Clara asks.

Just when I thought I was finished. But Cousin Clara is right. Some paint will make the house perfect.

Ivy Sue is very excited about her new house. It's big and beautiful. Just like Ivy Sue. All the walls are straight. All the nails, screws, and bolts are in place. And the roof will keep her dry when it's raining.

 What's the Word?

If you love Great Danes and a good mystery story, then read *The Invisible Dog* by Dick King-Smith. The story is about an imaginary Great Dane who comes to life.

I find an online article about the world's largest doghouse. It's covered with more than 100,000 dog biscuits. A company that makes dog biscuits built it. Imagine that.

Ivy Sue's house isn't *that* big. But it's big enough. To celebrate, Cousin Clara and I open two boxes of treats, one for Ivy Sue and one for Sophie. Ivy Sue's box holds 8 crunchy dog biscuits. Sophie's box holds 8 chewy cat treats. I plan to feed $\frac{3}{8}$ of Ivy Sue's treats to Ivy Sue. Cousin Clara wants to feed $\frac{2}{4}$ of Sophie's treats to Sophie. If we follow our plan, will Ivy Sue and Sophie get an equivalent number of treats?

Idea 1: Cousin Clara and I think about our problem. "We could use **fraction bars** to compare the fractions," she says.

Cousin Clara is right. "Comparing fraction bars would work," I say. "But I don't have a set of fraction bars handy."

Idea 2: "What about comparing **fraction lines** instead?" I ask.

Cousin Clara thinks about it. "This is a good idea. We could draw two lines. Then, we could divide one line into 4 equal parts and one line into 8 equal parts."

Idea 3: I have another idea. "We could use **fraction circles** to find the answer. Do you think that would be easier than drawing fraction lines?" I ask.

"Your idea is excellent," says Cousin Clara. "But drawing lines with equal parts may be easier than drawing circles with equal parts."

"Hmmm. I think you're right, Cousin Clara," I say. "Let's use fraction lines."

If we stick to our plan, will Ivy Sue and Sophie each get the same number of treats?

Cousin Clara and I have had our brownie treats. Ivy Sue and Sophie have had their treats, too. Now it's time for all of us to take a nap. If only I could get Ivy Sue off of my bed and into her new house!

WHAT COMES NEXT?

Have you ever tried to build a house for an animal? Perhaps you could work with an adult to build a house for a special kind of bird. It could be a barn owl.

A barn owl needs a house with a floor 18 inches long and 10 inches wide. The sides must be 15 to 18 inches high. There must be a hole on one side for the owl to get in. The hole must be at least 4 inches tall and 6 inches wide.

After your adult helper cuts the pieces of wood for the birdhouse, glue them together. Then, use nails or screws. This will help the birdhouse last longer.

Make a roof that will hang over the sides of the house. Put a $\frac{1}{4}$ inch space between the roof and the sides. This will let air move in and out. Drill $\frac{1}{4}$ inch holes in the floor to let rain drain away. Hang the birdhouse 12 to 18 feet above the ground. Then, wait for barn owls to arrive.

GLOSSARY

denominator: the part of a fraction below the fraction bar. It indicates how many parts make up the whole.

diameter: the length of a line going through the center of a circle.

equivalent fractions: two or more fractions that look different but have the same value.

fraction bars: a diagram or hands-on objects that show the relationships between fractional parts of a whole.

fraction circles: circles divided into equal parts.

fraction lines: diagrams that use points on a ruler to show the relationships between fractional parts of a whole.

fractions: parts of a whole.

irrigate: to bring a supply of water to a dry area to help crops grow.

line plot: data on a number line, with the symbol x or other mark to show frequency.

numerator: the part of a fraction above the fraction bar. It represents a number of parts out of the whole.

revolutions: sudden or complete changes; changes in government.

scribe: a writer.

shank: the long, straight part of a nail.

FURTHER READING

FICTION

Because of Winn-Dixie, by Kate DiCamillo, Candlewick Press, 2000

Fractions = Trouble!, by Claudia Mills, Farrar, Straus and Giroux, 2011

Shiloh, by Phyllis Reynolds Naylor, Atheneum Books for Young Readers, 1991

NONFICTION

Fractions, Decimals, and Percents, by David A. Adler, Holiday House, 2010

Piece = Part = Portion, by Scott Gifford, Tricycle Press, 2003

ADDITIONAL NOTES

The page references below provide answers to questions asked throughout the book. Questions whose answers will vary are not addressed.

Page 13: $\frac{1}{4}, \frac{1}{3}, \frac{1}{2}, \frac{2}{3}$

Page 15: I have three $\frac{1}{4}$ inch screws. I have the least amount of $\frac{2}{3}$ inch screws. I have the most of $\frac{3}{4}$ inch screws. Boxes A and C hold screws that are equivalent sizes. $\frac{2}{3} = \frac{4}{6}$

Page 17: $\frac{8}{10}$ and $\frac{12}{15}$

Page 19: $\frac{2}{4} = \frac{1}{2}$ The number of hand-printed and machine-printed books is the same.

Page 21: $\frac{2}{8} = \frac{1}{4}$, so more screws than nails fell out.

Page 22: $\frac{3}{4} = \frac{6}{8}$, so the $\frac{3}{4}$ inch nails are the widest.

Page 23: $\frac{3}{6} = \frac{6}{12}$, so each person has eaten the same amount of pizza.

Page 24: $\frac{2}{16} = \frac{1}{8}$, so each person has eaten the same number of brownies.

Pages 27–28: $\frac{2}{4} = \frac{4}{8}; \frac{4}{8} > \frac{3}{8}$, so, Sophie will get more treats.

INDEX

CONTENT CONSULTANT

David T. Hughes

David is an experienced mathematics teacher, writer, presenter, and adviser. He serves as a consultant for the Partnership for Assessment of Readiness for College and Careers. David has also worked as the Senior Program Coordinator for the Charles A. Dana Center at The University of Texas at Austin and was an editor and contributor for the *Mathematics Standards in the Classroom* series.

J 513.26 PERRITANO
Perritano, John.
Ivy Sue needs a house :
R2001083175 PALMETTO

ODC

Atlanta-Fulton Public Library